Cranbury
Public
Library

23 North Main St. • Cranbury, NJ 08512
(609) 655-0555

D1362134

SandCastle 3

Homonyms

An Ear Is Not an Ear

Kelly Doudna

ABDO
Publishing Company

Published by SandCastle™, an imprint of ABDO Publishing Company, 4940 Viking Drive, Edina, Minnesota 55435.

Copyright © 2002 by Abdo Consulting Group, Inc. International copyrights reserved in all countries. No part of this book may be reproduced in any form without written permission from the publisher. SandCastle™ is a trademark and logo of Abdo Publishing Company.

Printed in the United States.

Photo credits: Digital Vision, Eyewire Images, John Foxx Images, PhotoDisc, Rubberball Productions

Library of Congress Cataloging-in-Publication Data

Doudna, Kelly, 1963-
    An ear is not an ear / Kelly Doudna.
       p. cm. -- (Homonyms)
    Includes index.
    Summary: Photographs and simple text introduce homonyms, words that are spelled and sound the same but have different meanings.
    ISBN 1-57765-788-8
       1. English language--Homonyms--Juvenile literature. [1. English language--Homonyms.] I. Title.

PE1595 .D73 2002
428.1--dc21
2001053309

The SandCastle concept, content, and reading method have been reviewed and approved by a national advisory board including literacy specialists, librarians, elementary school teachers, early childhood education professionals, and parents.

Let Us Know

After reading the book, SandCastle would like you to tell us your stories about reading. What is your favorite page? Was there something hard that you needed help with? Share the ups and downs of learning to read. We want to hear from you! To get posted on the Abdo Publishing Company Web site, send us email at:

sandcastle@abdopub.com

About SandCastle™

Nonfiction books for the beginning reader

- Basic concepts of phonics are incorporated with integrated language methods of reading instruction. Most words are short, and phrases, letter sounds, and word sounds are repeated.

- Book levels are based on the ATOS™ for Books formula. Other considerations for readability include the number of words in each sentence, the number of characters in each word, and word lists based on curriculum frameworks.

- Full-color photography reinforces word meanings and concepts.

- "Words I Can Read" list at the end of each book teaches basic elements of grammar, helps the reader recognize the words in the text, and builds vocabulary.

- Reading levels are indicated by the number of flags on the castle.

SandCastle uses the following definitions for this series:

- Homographs: words that are spelled the same but sound different and have different meanings. *Easy memory tip: "-graph"= same look*

- Homonyms: words that are spelled and sound the same but have different meanings. *Easy memory tip: "-nym"= same name*

- Homophones: words that sound alike but are spelled differently and have different meanings. *Easy memory tip: "-phone"= sound alike*

Look for more SandCastle books in these three reading levels:

Level 1 (one flag)	**Level 2** (two flags)	**Level 3** (three flags)

Grades Pre-K to K 5 or fewer words per page	**Grades K to 1** 5 to 10 words per page	**Grades 1 to 2** 10 to 15 words per page

glasses   glasses

Homonyms are words that are spelled and sound the same but have different meanings.

A baby cow is a calf.

Calves live on farms.

The backs of our legs are our calves.

We hide under the umbrella.

The capital of the United States is Washington, D.C.

This is the White House.

My name is Susan.

Every name starts with a capital letter.

This rooster lives on a farm.

He crows every morning.

Crows are black birds.

They are big and make a cawing sound.

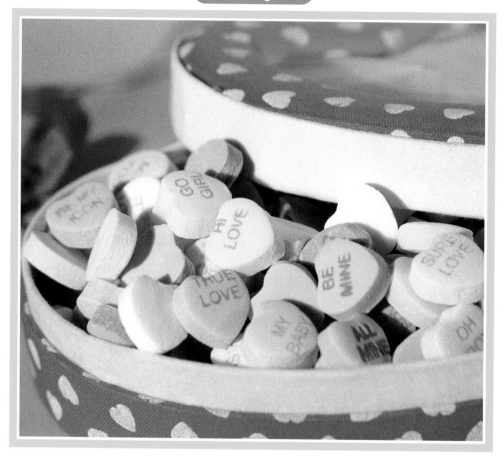

February 14th is the date of Valentine's Day.

I like to eat candy hearts.

Our grandparents brought us to the park for a play date.

Mom and Dad have friends over.

We cook out on the back deck.

We have a deck of cards.

We know how to play several games.

My down pillows are stuffed with feathers.

They are soft.

Dad took me to the playground.

I slid down the pole.

Dad took me golfing.

He let me drive the golf cart.

Dad uses a hammer to drive the nail into the board.

I will buy this truck.

I count my money to see if I have enough.

It is Halloween.

What costume do I wear?

(Count Dracula)

Words I Can Read

Nouns

A noun is a person, place, or thing

backs (BAKSS) p. 7
birds (BURDZ) p. 11
board (BORD) p. 19
calf (KAF) p. 6
calves (KAVZ) pp. 6, 7
capital (KAP-uh-tuhl)
  p. 8
cards (KARDZ) p. 15
costume (KOSS-toom)
  p. 21
cow (KOU) p. 6
crows (KROHZ) p. 11
date (DAYT) p. 12
deck (DEK) pp. 14, 15
down pillows
  (DOUN PIL-ohz) p. 16
farm (FARM) p. 10
farms (FARMZ) p. 6

feathers (FETH-urz)
  p. 16
friends (FRENDZ) p. 14
games (GAYMZ) p. 15
glasses (GLASS-iz) p. 4
golf cart (GOLF KART)
  p. 18
grandparents
  (GRAND-pa-ruhntss)
  p. 13
hammer (HAM-ur) p. 19
hearts (HARTSS) p. 12
homonyms
  (HOM-uh-nimz) p. 5
legs (LEGZ) p. 7
letter (LET-ur) p. 9
meanings (MEE-ningz)
  p. 5

money (MUHN-ee) p. 20
morning (MOR-ning)
  p. 10
nail (NAYL) p. 19
name (NAYM) p. 9
park (PARK) p. 13
play date
  (PLAY DAYT) p. 13
playground
  (PLAY-ground) p. 17
pole (POHL) p. 17
rooster (ROO-stur)
  p. 10
sound (SOUND) p. 11
truck (TRUHK) p. 20
umbrella
  (uhm-BREL-uh) p. 7
words (WURDZ) p. 5

Proper Nouns

A proper noun is the name of a
person, place, or thing

Count Dracula
  (KOUNT
  DRAK-yoo-luh) p. 21
Dad (DAD)
  pp. 14, 17, 18, 19
February
  (FEB-roo-er-ee) p. 12

Halloween
  (hal-oh-EEN) p. 21
Mom (MOM) p. 14
Susan (SOO-zuhn) p. 9
United States
  (yoo-NITE-ed
  STATESS) p. 8

Valentine's Day
  (VAL-uhn-tinez DAY)
  p. 12
Washington, D.C.
  (WOSH-ing-tuhn
  DEE SEE) p. 8
White House
  (WITE HOUSS) p. 8

22

Pronouns

A pronoun is a word that replaces a noun

he (HEE) pp. 10, 18

I (EYE) pp. 12, 17, 20, 21

it (IT) p. 21

me (MEE) pp. 17, 18

that (THAT) p. 5

they (THAY) pp. 11, 16

this (THISS) p. 8

us (UHSS) p. 13

we (WEE) pp. 7, 14, 15

what (WUHT) p. 21

Verbs

A verb is an action or being word

are (AR) pp. 5, 7, 11, 16

brought (BRAWT) p. 13

buy (BYE) p. 20

cook (KUK) p. 14

count (KOUNT) p. 20

crows (KROHZ) p. 10

do (DOO) p. 21

drive (DRIVE) pp. 18, 19

eat (EET) p. 12

golfing (GOLF-ing)
 p. 18

have (HAV)
 pp. 5, 14, 15, 20

hide (HIDE) p. 7

is (IZ) pp. 6, 8, 9, 12, 21

know (NOH) p. 15

let (LET) p. 18

like (LIKE) p. 12

live (LIV) p. 6

lives (LIVZ) p. 10

make (MAYK) p. 11

play (PLAY) p. 15

see (SEE) p. 20

slid (SLID) p. 17

sound (SOUND) p. 5

spelled (SPELD) p. 5

starts (STARTSS) p. 9

stuffed (STUHFT) p. 16

took (TUK) pp. 17, 18

uses (YOOZ-ez) p. 19

wear (WAIR) p. 21

will (WIL) p. 20

Adjectives

An adjective describes something

baby (BAY-bee) p. 6
back (BAK) p. 14
big (BIG) p. 11
black (BLAK) p. 11
candy (KAN-dee) p. 12
capital (KAP-uh-tuhl)
   p. 9

cawing (KAW-ing)
   p. 11
different (DIF-ur-uhnt)
   p. 5
enough (i-NUF) p. 20
every (EV-ree) pp. 9, 10
my (MYE)
   pp. 9, 16, 20

our (OUR) pp. 7, 13
same (SAYM) p. 5
several (SEV-ur-uhl)
   p. 15
soft (SAWFT) p. 16
this (THISS) pp. 10, 20

Adverbs

An adverb tells how, when, or where
something happens

out (OUT) p. 14

over (OH-vur) p. 14

24

CRANBURY PUBLIC LIBRARY

3 9380 00049475 8

CRANBURY PUBLIC LIBRARY
23 North Main Street
Cranbury, NJ 08512

OC 4 05